Acknowledgements

D1128126

Many people must be thanked for their help in this book's becoming a book and not sim... computer!

I thank Tina Taylor McEwen for the shadow work embroidery designs and for most of the art in this book, which she began working on more than a year ago! She has worked with me to illustrate the "how-to-do-it" section. Her work is beautiful and she is such a pleasure to work with. I would like to thank Diane Zinser for the stitching and painting of the designs. She was assisted by Terry Blue. A special thanks goes to Joia Johnson for the book design and the layout.

Mary, my sister, Kathy McMakin, Judith Dobson, Kathy Pearce, Becky Lambert, Yulanda Gilliam, Sandra Parton, Scott Wright, Westa Chandler, Lillie Jones, Aritta York, Margaret Taylor, Ashley Pearce, Amelia Johanson, and Kathy Willoughby—I thank you.

Margaret Boyles' assistance was needed in several areas. Since she is one of my very best friends, I thank her for her help in writing this book and for her friendship, encouragement and support throughout the years. What would I do without Margaret's sweet voice on the other end of the telephone? She is a marvelous counselor and understands things which baffle me.

I thank Mildred Turner for sending her section on shadow work embroidery, giving directions for stitching from the front of the work. Mildred Turner's friendship and love has been invaluable to me throughout the last number of years. She always stands ready to help and to give of her talent when I need her. In this book in particular, it was she who insisted on sending her already written shadow work embroidery instructions which I am sure she had intended to publish. Her words were, "Martha, you are writing the book. We don't need but one. Just take my directions and use them." Her artist, Rebekah Russell illustrated Mildred's section.

My mother, Anna Ruth Dicus Campbell, helps me with all of my business and personal endeavors. From cooking for my schools, to baby sitting, to giving sound advice, to making collection calls, to traveling to shows with me—she is always there for every book that I shall ever write. Every success in life that I will ever have, I give God the first credit, because it is truly His. After thanking God, I give thanks and appreciation to my mother. Without her lifetime of 100% support and sacrifice, I certainly would not be where I am today.

My boys are just about grown now; probably most people would say that they certainly are grown. John has a beautiful Christian bride, Suzanne. They are in seminary school at Columbia Bible College in Columbia, South Carolina. They will be missionaries in Africa one day. By the way, Suzanne is a nurse. Mark is in dental school and will be married soon to another precious Christian girl, Sherry Ann Greene. Camp also is engaged to a wonderful Christian girl, Laura Elizabeth Welch. They are finishing degrees at Arizona State University and will be married after graduation. Camp will be entering my business at that time and yes, he has learned to sew! Jeff has graduated in hotel and restaurant management from Florida International University. He is happily employed by the Marriott Corporation here in Huntsville. Last Valentine's day he became engaged to Angela Cataldo, a lovely Christian girl. So I am truly blessed to have seen my boys go from swinging and swaying like teen-agers do, to becoming fabulous men who have chosen lovely women with whom to share their lives. Thank you God!

Always, my love and thanks goes to Joe Ross Pullen, my husband. Without his financial support and complete belief in my business abilities, there would be no Martha Pullen Co., Inc., no *Sew Beautiful*, and no *Pageants & Talent*. I would never have had the courage to have taken such a risk and to have done any of these things. He has always believed in me more than I believed in myself. He has always encouraged me to keep on trying when I wanted to quit. I love him and I thank him.

February 23, 1976, Joanna Emma Joyce Pullen was born. After having been blessed with four healthy boys, I absolutely did not believe that my perfect baby was a girl! My lifelong love of sewing and needlework began to spin in my head as never before! I finally had a little girl to sew for! I learned to smock, French sew (by machine mostly) and shadow embroider. She has loved wearing my creations and my embroidery. When she was a little girl she loved coming to the shop and demonstrating button holes on the sewing machines and twirling around to show her "swish" dresses. She loves modeling in our fashion shows all over the country as well as in our magazine, *Sew Beautiful*. She has been the sweetest and kindest little girl that I could ever have dreamed of having. If Joanna hadn't been born, I don't know that this business would have ever been created. So, when I write any book or publish any magazine about embroidery, beautiful children's clothing, or smocking, I will have to ultimately thank Joanna. All of these creations have really been with her in mind. I thank her for everything! I dedicate this book to Joanna with at least three million tons of love!

Table of Contents

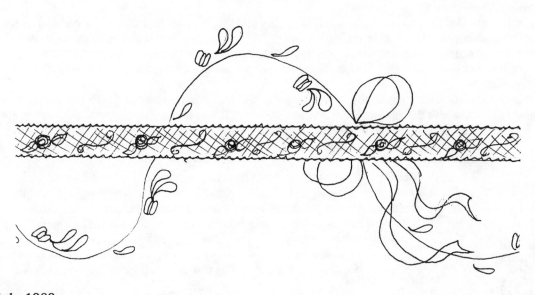

Martha Pullen Company, Inc.
518 Madison Street   Huntsville, Al
35801
1-205-533-9586

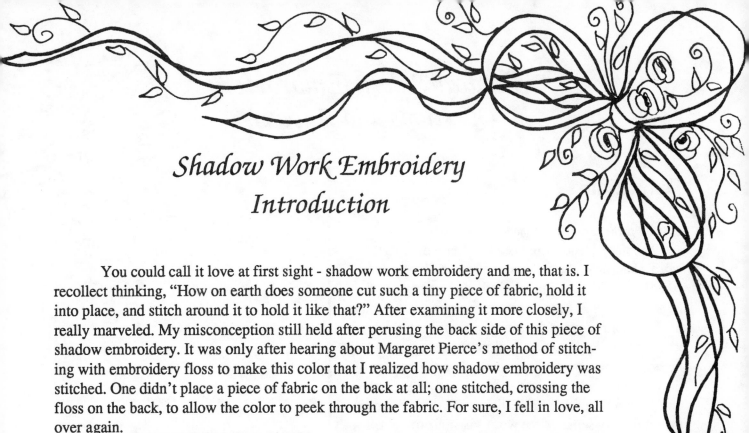

Shadow Work Embroidery
Introduction

You could call it love at first sight - shadow work embroidery and me, that is. I recollect thinking, "How on earth does someone cut such a tiny piece of fabric, hold it into place, and stitch around it to hold it like that?" After examining it more closely, I really marveled. My misconception still held after perusing the back side of this piece of shadow embroidery. It was only after hearing about Margaret Pierce's method of stitching with embroidery floss to make this color that I realized how shadow embroidery was stitched. One didn't place a piece of fabric on the back at all; one stitched, crossing the floss on the back, to allow the color to peek through the fabric. For sure, I fell in love, all over again.

It had been many years since I had made crewel embroidery for all my Christmas gifts and I was surprised at how much I had forgotten. After learning that the method was teachable, I certainly figured that it would be difficult and too hard for me. Remember, I am basically a sewing machine person, not a needleworker. However, all around me, embroiderers exclaimed that shadow embroidery was the easiest form to learn. These ideas came from several different people.

At one of my Schools of Art Fashion many years ago, Mary Hale came to teach the "easy method of shadow embroidery" and so I took the class from her. Much to my amazement, it was terribly easy and beautiful also. Even a rusty, crewel needleworker could make beautiful shadow embroidery on the first try. I would never make this statement about other forms of surface embroidery! Mary Hale and I wrote a book entitled *Shadow Work Embroidery Made Easy.* That book has been out of print for some time now.

Shadow embroidery is certainly not new. I taught shadow embroidery in my shop for several years; each time I was amazed at how easily my students learned this form of embroidery. We only taught one 3 hour class because everyone caught on so quickly. And they all loved it very, very much. Believe it or not, almost 100% of all the students were pleased with the beauty of the first project!

In the magazine, *Sew Beautiful,* the whole world has fallen in love with Judith Dobson's lovely shadow embroidery combined with other forms of surface embroidery. For those of you who think you can only dream of stitching such exquisite pieces of shadow work, this easy, teacher-version shadow embroidery book is for you.

Shadow Work Embroidery
Questions and Answers

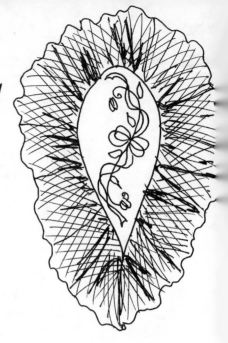

Definition

I. What is the definition of shadow work embroidery?

Webster's Handy College Dictionary defines the word shadow in the following manner: **Shad' ow** (shad' o) 1, the dark image of a body intercepting the light. 2, shade. 3, an inseparable companion. All three of these definitions make sense in describing shadow work embroidery. Since I think of shadow embroidery in terms of being easy, I especially like the portion of the definition which says a shadow is an "inseparable companion." Another interesting word to examine (in the dictionary sense of the word) is **shad'ow graph**- a picture produced by casting a shadow, as of the hands, on a screen.

The "real" definition of shadow work embroidery is "a closed herringbone stitch." Worked left to right between somewhat parallel lines, the color of the floss shows through from the back to give a shadow effect. The floss, crossed on the back of the fabric, can be stitched from either the front or the back of the piece. Directions will be given for both; however, my preference is to stitch from the back.

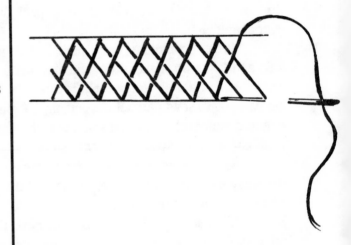

Type of Needle for Shadow Embroidery

II. What kind of needle should I use for shadow embroidery?

The general preference for needle size is a #26 tapestry needle. It is large enough to make a hole in the fabric which can be seen for the next stitch placement. The dull point of the tapestry needle is excellent for this stitch. If you prefer a needle with a point, try a #6 crewel needle. Many skilled embroiderers working in very tiny stitches will use an even smaller crewel needle such as #7, 8, or 9. The best needles for shadow embroidery are Margaret Boyles' Fine English Needles. These needles are the best available in the world. Don't waste your time with a bad needle. The crewel needles, all sizes, come in packages of 18; the tapestry needles

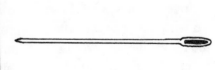

4

are in packages of 12. Write to Margaret for a catalogue at the following address: Margaret and Co., 200 Wedgeway, Atlanta, GA 30350 (404-992-0214).

Needle Tips for Surface Embroidery

III. Do you have any tips about needles which would help me with my surface embroidery, such as bullion rosebuds?

Margaret Boyles and Judith Dobson feel that the shape of Margaret's #10 crewel needle makes it easier to pull a thread through for a beautiful bullion knot. Margaret uses this #10 crewel needle for all surface embroidery using one strand of floss. If you prefer another needle or if you are using more strands of floss, try her #9 crewel needles. By the way, crewel needles have short eyes and pointed tips.

Margaret
Boyles'

Fine French
Needles

Unusual Floss for Shadow Embroidery

IV. Do you know of any unusual floss which makes shadow embroidery unique?

Margaret Boyles has discovered a variegated, 6-strand, cotton floss which makes gorgeous shadow embroidery and also fabulous bullion rosebuds. The variegation is shorter than the usual variegated floss; the colors flow together in a very elegant manner. This imparts a very delicate and subtle shading to fine embroidery. The floss comes in a 20-yard skein for approximately $2. At present time there are twenty shades; more are expected shortly.

Kinds of Embroidery Floss

V. What kind of floss do you use for regular shadow work embroidery?

DMC and Susan Bates are excellent choices.

Number of Strands for Shadow Work Embroidery

VI. How many strands of floss do you use?

Usually, one strand of floss is used for shadow work embroidery.

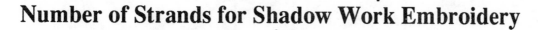

5

Hoops for Shadow Embroidery

VII. What kind of hoop is best?

My preference is a 4" or 5" plastic hoop with a screw closing.

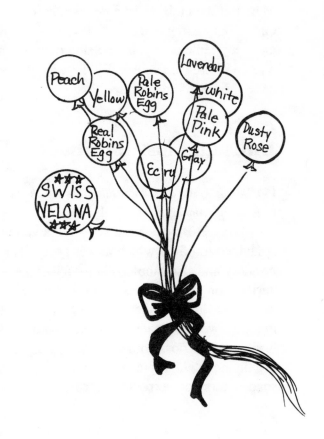

Choices of Fabric for Shadow Work Embroidery

VIII. What kinds of fabrics lend themselves to shadow work embroidery nicely?

Several types of fabrics are wonderful. Swiss Nelona is one of the very best. It is 100% Swiss cotton batiste and is available exclusively from Martha Pullen, Co., Inc. The reason I love Nelona for shadow work embroidery is that it has a little bit of body. Some Swiss batiste, such as Oriunda, is much thinner and the holes are too big after the needle travels through the fabric. White is everybody's favorite for shadow embroidery; however, absolutely gorgeous work has been done on every pastel color of Nelona. These are ecru, lavender, pale robin's egg blue, pale blue, pale pink, gray and pale peach.

Another favorite of mine is handkerchief linen in white and ecru. Imperial batiste or Wistful batiste are excellent choices in the poly/cotton domestic fabrics. They are very easy to work on. Swiss organdy or Italian organdy are lovely also. When you work on organdy, you must be very careful to make your stitches precise. Each stitch really shows when you are working with this fabric.

Antiqueing Fabric

IX. Where can I get a really "antiqued" Swiss batiste color? I make dolls and I love the really old looking colors.

I have good news for you. You can dye the palest Swiss colors with coffee and have the most marvelous antiqued colors. The formula for dying batiste is 1 cup of coffee with 2 tablespoons of vinegar in it. Experiment with the colors of Swiss batiste. Here are the specifics for using Swiss Nelona pale colors.
1. Pale Peach Swiss Nelona- This color dyes to a gorgeous, yellowish peach.

2. Pale Robin's Egg Swiss Nelona-Believe it or not, this dyes to an antiqued, beautiful mint green.

3. Pale Gray Swiss Nelona-This dyes to a darker gray.

4. Pale Pink Swiss Nelona-This dyes to an antiqued, pale pink.

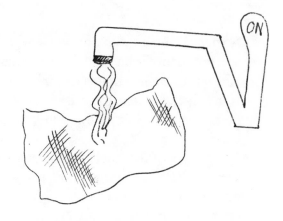

Dyeing Fabrics

X. Tell me exactly how I dye white or the palest colors of Swiss batiste.

1. Take one cup of coffee, warm or cold, with two tablespoons of vinegar in it. If you are dyeing a large piece of fabric, you will want to make more than one cup of the mixture.

2. **VERY IMPORTANT**- Thoroughly wet your fabric with water before placing it into the coffee.

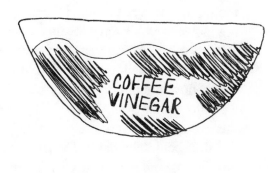

3. Leave the fabric in the coffee mixture for several minutes.

4. Remove the fabric and rinse with water until all of the coffee-colored mixture comes out.

5. Check your color. Do you want it darker? If so, repeat the procedure.

6. After getting the right color, let the fabric dry before pressing it. When you press wet fabric after dyeing it in this manner, you may get streaks.

7. Do you want fabric which really looks 100 years old? In this case, press it while it is still wet. It actually stains it in a very antique manner when pressed from a completely wet state.

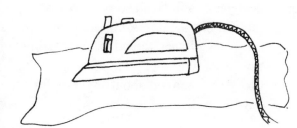

Garments for Shadow Work Embroidery

XI. Where do you put shadow work embroidery?

I think shadow work embroidery is beautiful on almost anything! What could be more beautiful than a white on white shadow work design trailing from the yoke to the bottom of the skirt of a christening gown? For yokes on little girls' dresses, nothing is more elegant. I especially love shadow work on collars of all types for little girls, boys, and ladies. Embroider your own insertions rather than spending $15 to $20 per yard on Swiss or Chinese, handmade insertions.

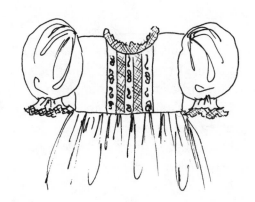

A friend of mine, who does not sew, came by my shop and fell in love with shadow work embroidery. She happens to be the number one interior designer in Huntsville. Her reaction was, "I have to have that design on a boudoir pillow with lots of lace for my bedroom."

One of the cutest shadow work outfits I have seen was store bought with shadow stitching on the bodice. That is another advantage of shadow work embroidery or any embroidery, for that matter. It can be stitched on purchased outfits. You don't have to look too far to discover the delicious patterns in the smocking industry which have lovely collars just perfect for shadow stitching. Almost any yoke or collar lends itself beautifully to shadow work. One of my favorite ideas for shadow stitching is to smock a collar leaving about 2" in the center front. Stitch shadow work embroidery there. Something very pretty would be to stitch a few of the alphabet letters there. The finishing touch is a bullion rosebud nestled in each letter.

Shadow work embroidery does not have to be fancy and lacy. It can be very tailored. In the Spring 1989 *Sew Beautiful*, Diane Zinser designed a small, navy blue anchor with gold metallic chain. This was placed on a very tailored collar of white linen; the blouse was worn with navy shorts. Several of the designers have taken story book ideas such as trains, rabbits, bears, houses, children, and other simple outlines and stitched them in shadow stitching. Of course, my very favorite of all is shadow work embroidered bows. Put them on about anything for little girls or ladies.

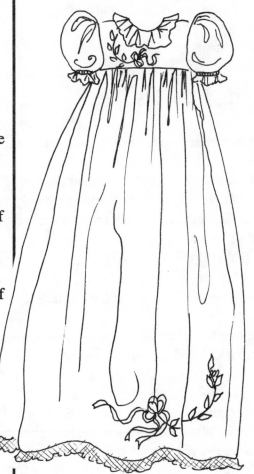

A Thimble or Not?

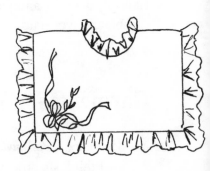

XII. Should I use a thimble?

This is entirely up to you. I used to use a thimble for all hand stitching before I began smocking. I then discarded my thimble; my mother and my Aunt Chris must not know about this fact! Since you are only using one strand of floss, you most likely won't poke holes in your fingers. Please try it both ways. Either way will be fine!

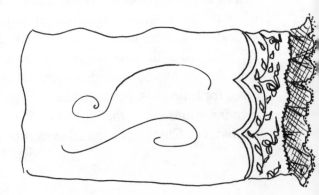

Using More Than One Strand of Floss

XIII. Do you ever use more than one strand of floss?

     The general rule of thumb is one strand. If you are doing shadow work embroidery on a baby quilt, you may use more. If you are doing shadow work embroidery on a heavier fabric, such as broadcloth, you will have to use more than one. One reason heavier fabrics aren't used more is that the herringbone on the back will not show through; however it is still a pretty form of embroidery even when you can't see the stitches from the back.

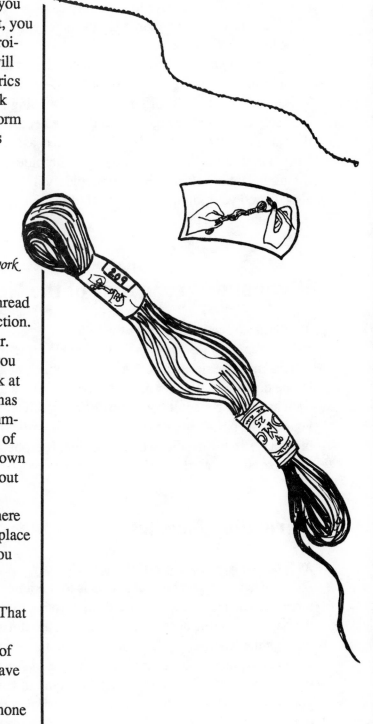

Putting Floss on Grain

XIV. How do I prepare my embroidery floss for shadow work embroidery so that it is put on grain properly?

     Do you know that all thread has a grain? Thread for your sewing machine pulls off in only one direction. The grain comes off the spool in the correct manner. Since we have only given DMC colors, I will tell you how to get the correct grain using DMC floss. Look at the two paper wraps on the embroidery floss. One has the round DMC symbol. The other has the color number and a picture of two hands pulling the floss out of the package. Place your left hand on the floss as shown on the picture. With your right hand, pull the floss out of the package as shown on the picture. The place where you cut your floss will always be the end where you place the knot in your thread. Since you don't place a knot in thread for stitching, this will be the end you leave hanging before you begin your stitching.

     Before shadow stitching, I separate all the strands. Go ahead and place a knot on the cut end. That way, you won't forget which end will be the "non stitching end." Since shadow embroidery uses lots of floss, you will be surprised how quickly you will have to thread up again.

     Now for the big question. What if the telephone rings or the doorbell rings or you have to jump up to rescue a child, or dog, or whatever, before you get the knots in those cut ends? Is the situation lost forever?

No, not at all. Here is a tip I learned from Dr. Cornelia Anderson which I would like to share with you. One end of the floss "blooms" more than the other end. The cut end of the floss (where you are going to place your knot) does not fuzz out as much as the other end of the floss. Sometimes you have to look very carefully to see which one has bloomed more than the other end. You place the knot on the less fuzzy end.

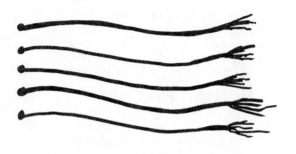

When you are threading large needles, it usually doesn't matter which end goes through the needle first. The situation is entirely different when threading #10 crewels or smaller! I suggest threading the needle with the cut end or the less fuzzy of the two. It's easier. Then I slip it through the needle and out the embroidery hoop if I am beginning shadow work embroidery. If you have already tied your knot, then cut it off, thread your needle and tie it again.

Right and Wrong Side of the Needle

XV. Do needles have a right and wrong side?

Yes, they do! Have you ever wondered why sewing machine needles only go into the machine slot in one direction? Wonder no more. They do have a right and wrong side. It you have difficulty threading your needle before beginning your shadow work embroidery, flip the needle to the other side. It probably will be easier to work with!

Threading Needles

XVI. Is there any easy way to thread a needle?

There are several tricks. One is to use a needle threader. The best trick I can share with you is to wet the back side of the needle before pushing the thread through the front. This works on hand sewing or on sewing machine needles. Try it. You'll like it! Another tip for threading a needle is to take the strand of floss in your hand and fold about an inch of one end over the thickest part of the needle. Pinch the strand tightly around the needle using your thumb and index finger. Pull the needle away from the floss. While you are still holding the pinched floss, push the eye of the needle toward it to pass the floss through.

Right and Wrong Sides of Fabric

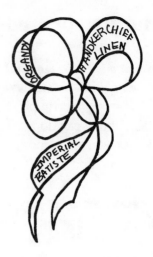

XVII. Does batiste have a right and wrong side? How about organdy?

Technically they might in some cases. Some people say the sheen on Swiss Nelona is prettier on one side. Some people say the same thing about Imperial. I have never been able to see this. Usually I can't tell a right side on organdy either. It has been said, "If you flip a fabric over several times and can't tell about the right and wrong side, it probably doesn't have one." I have always used that story about laces and this type of fabric.

Length of Floss

XVIII. How long should my piece of floss be for shadow work embroidery?

My suggestion is to use a piece of floss about 18" to 22" long. Any shorter runs out too quickly; any longer gets worn out. It is some trouble to weave the ends to finish shadow work, so I don't like to work with too short a piece.

18 - 22 inches

Avoiding Fabric Stretching

XIX. What can I do to keep my fabric from stretching as I move my hoop over the design?

There are several ways to do this. My favorite suggestion is to wrap the inner ring of the plastic hoop with gauze you get in the medical aids section of any drug store. This pads the hoop somewhat and helps keep the fabric from stretching. Just wrap the inner ring and place a few stitches to keep it from slipping off as you work.

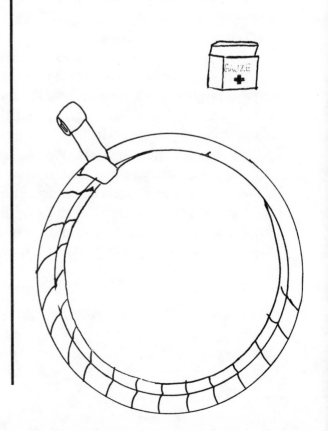

Enlarging or Reducing a Design

XX. Sometimes I see a beautiful design; however it is too large or too small. How do I size my artwork to fit my garment?

The wonderful photostat machines which are available today can do magic to a pattern. Go to your local photostat store and have them enlarge or reduce your design. You might take color books, embroidery books, etc. to make a pattern out of something really large. There are other methods for enlarging using graph paper. This method is tedious and time consuming. With the marvels of photostat machines, I think the best way to use your time is in your stitching rather than trying to enlarge the old-fashioned way.

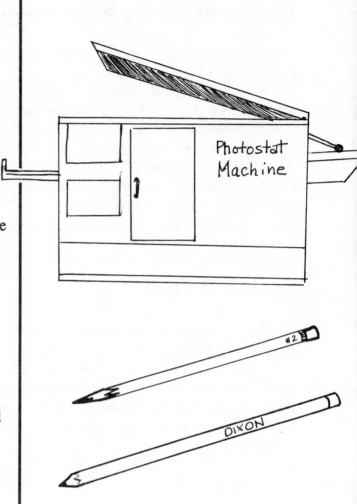

Photostat Machine

Tools to Trace the Design

XXI. What do I use to trace my design onto the fabric?

My preference for the tracing tool is a #2 or a Dixon pencil. The water soluble pens do not work well because the lines are not exact enough. The Dixon pencil works just like a pencil, but it is water soluble.

Transferring a Design to Fabric

XXII. How do I trace my design?

If you are stitching from the back of the fabric, you must trace the design once onto the top of the fabric. Then, go to a light source, such as a window or a light box and trace the design again through to the back of the fabric. If you use a window, just attach the pattern and your fabric to the window with a piece of masking tape or scotch tape. Often, you can use a copier to copy a design onto a thin paper; flip the paper and trace onto the back side of your fabric. Sometimes, the fabric is thin enough for you to stitch from the back with the lines peeking through from the front.

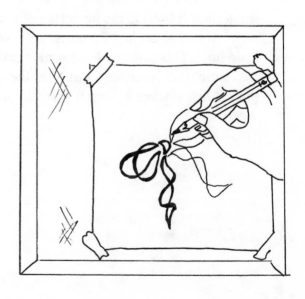

Special Tricks for Transferring the Design

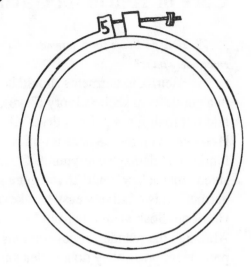

XXIII. Is there an easy way to trace exact lines onto fabric?

I think it is easier to trace the design onto the fabric if you put the fabric into the embroidery hoop before tracing it. If this is something you would like to try, the wrong side of the fabric will be the side showing when you place the hoop on the table for tracing. Remember, if you do the shadow work from the wrong side (as is my preferred way), the design is traced onto the wrong side of the fabric.

If you have used your hoop to trace the design, you will need to place your traced design on the top of the hoop before you begin stitching.

Positioning the Fabric, Design and Hoop

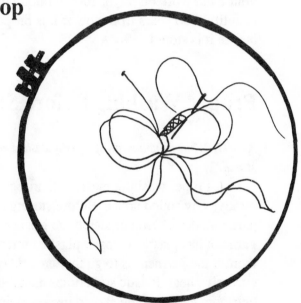

XXIV. Exactly how will the hoop and the traced design look before I begin stitching?

The outer portion of the hoop with the screw will be on the outside; the inner ring of the hoop (the one you have wrapped with gauze) will be on the inside of the fabric. The wrong side of the fabric with the pencil markings on it will be on the top surface of the embroidery hoop.

Pressing Your Work

XXV. How do I press my work after it is done?

Never let the iron touch your surface of your shadow work embroidery. After the stitching is completed, wash your work with Ivory soap or hand soap in a little pump bottle. The pencil markings or Dixon pencil should be removed completely with this washing. Lay your work on a towel and roll very gently to remove the excess water. Place a white towel on your ironing board. Place the damp piece, embroidery side down, on this towel. Place a piece of batiste or other clean white fabric on top of the embroidery. Now you are ready to gently press your work.

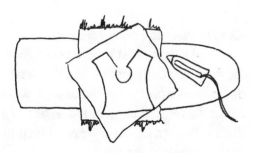

Care of Heirloom Garments

XXVI. How do I care for a garment which has shadow work embroidery on it?

Heirloom garments should be washed by hand in a gentle soap such as Ivory Flakes. They should be laid flat to dry, not put in a dryer. **Do Not Dry Clean Heirloom Garments** because this tends to yellow fabrics and damage everything! Cleaners do not understand embroidery at all! If you get a stain on your garment, it is relatively easy to take out by soaking it in Heirloom Soak available from Martha Pullen Co., Inc. Although the wonderful poly cottons are great for permanent press, they do not clean as easily as 100% cotton. My preference is to use heirloom fabrics (100% Swiss Nelona) on garments which will have a lot of your hand work on them. 100% cotton will be just as beautiful 100 years from now if it is properly washed before it is stored.

Proper Washing Before Storing

XXVII. What do you mean "properly washed before it is stored?"

Proper washing means a thorough cleaning to remove any soiled areas. Before storing an heirloom garment, do not iron or starch the garment. If the garment has plastic snaps or plastic buttons, remove them if the garment is to go into an attic or garage with excessive heat. Plastic sometimes melts. In a truly heirloom garment you should use pearl buttons and stainless steel snaps covered with batiste circles. If Christian Dior covers his snaps, why shouldn't we?

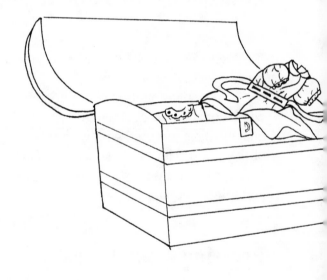

Starting and Ending Off

XXVIII. How do I finish my work?

As with most needlework, do not put knots on the back of your work. When you have used your floss or finished a portion of the design, weave the floss along the outside edge of the design. Take care not to disturb the herringbone weave which makes the shadow peek through to the front.

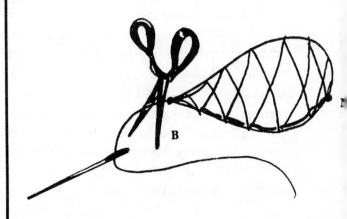

Ripping Out

XXVIV. What do I do if I make a mistake or if my work isn't the right color?

Most beautiful needlework appears perfect. Don't believe for one minute that some of the stitches haven't had to be taken out. If you make a mistake in color, carefully pull out the stitches. Choose another color. If you have a messy look when turning circles which has one side very much larger than the other, carefully pull out the stitches and plan more carefully when to start increasing the stitches on the long side and decreasing the stitches on the short side. Remember, almost everybody has to do some ripping. To take out shadow work embroidery, unthread the needle before removing any unwanted stitches. Whenever possible use the eye rather than the point of the needle to loosen unwanted stitches.

If you are working on fine batiste, little holes may show after taking out the stitches. Don't worry. Stitch over them. After your work is finished, you will first remove your tracing lines of either pencil or Dixon pencil. After removing your tracing lines your fabric will be damp. Steaming the fabric with an iron, embroidery side down, will close up any holes which are still apparent.

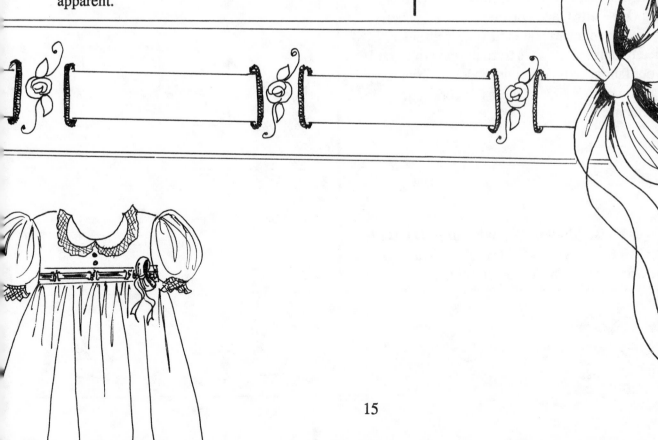

Extra Useful Tips Before Beginning Your Work

I. Test Stitches: Before you begin your work, you might want to make some test stitches using your chosen colors and your chosen fabric. This is especially true if you are changing colors of a design or if you have made your own design. When you see changes you would like to make in your shadow embroidery, you will not have to pull out stitches and leave holes in your fabric.

II. Planning Fabric: Allow a little extra fabric when you are doing shadow embroidery. You will need extra fabric for handling.

III. Always Complete Your Embroidery Before Cutting Out Your Garment Piece: Never, never, never, cut out your garment until your embroidery is completely finished. Always trace the pattern piece onto your fabric, complete your shadow embroidery, wash your work, dry it, and press it before cutting out your garment.

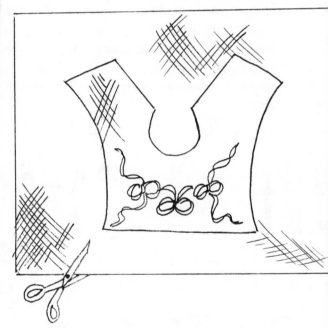

IV. Never Finish Shadow Work Embroidery With Knots On The Back: The final finish is always woven. See the complete instructions in this book.

Instructions
For Shadow Work Embroidery (Method Number 1)

This method, which is my favorite, makes the stitches from the wrong side of the fabric. When the fabric is loaded into the hoop, the wrong side of the garment will be facing out. The design is traced onto that side. The stitches are rather like "sewing" with a bite taken out of the top of the design and a bite taken out of the bottom. The stitch is a closed herringbone stitch. The reason that I personally like this method best is because it is the easiest, I think. Other people prefer working from the front of the finished piece.

Steps For Method Number 1

1. Trace your design onto the wrong side of the fabric. If you are using an alphabet, for instance, be certain that the design is "wrong side out" because you are working from the back. If your design is not given "wrong side out" in the design book and you want to use this method. Using a photostat machine, copy the design onto a clear plastic sheet like you would use for an overhead projector. This is called a transparency. Flip the transparency over. Run a copy on paper this time. It will be reversed properly.

2. Insert the fabric into the embroidery hoop.

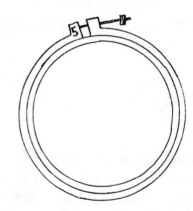

3. Cut a piece of embroidery floss approximately 18" to 22" long. Remember to knot the cut end, although you will later cut that knot away. Shadow work embroidery never has knots on the work. This knot is to remind you to stitch with the proper grain of the floss.

18 - 22 inches

17

4. There are two ways of placing the loose end (the knotted end of the floss) while you stitch your shadow embroidery. **(1.)** The first is to lay the end (rather a long one) outside the embroidery hoop and close the hoop over it. This gives you plenty of floss to later load into the needle to weave and finish off this end of the work. After securing the floss into the hoop, you are now ready to begin your shadow stitching. **(2.)** The second way is to bring your knot up through the circle of fabric as far away from your first stitching as possible. The reason I do not like this way as well as the first is that sometimes there is not enough embroidery floss "tail" to easily thread into the needle and to weave to finish.

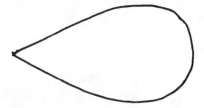

5. Following the illustrations given using a leaf shape, begin your stitching.

6. Thread below the needle, bring your needle down at (A) and up at (B). Pull through.

7. Move down. Thread above the needle, put your needle down at (C) and up at (B). Move into the exact same hole as your needle made on the first bite at (B). In order to easily remember whether the thread is above or below the needle, see the "Cat And The Courthouse Story" which follows.

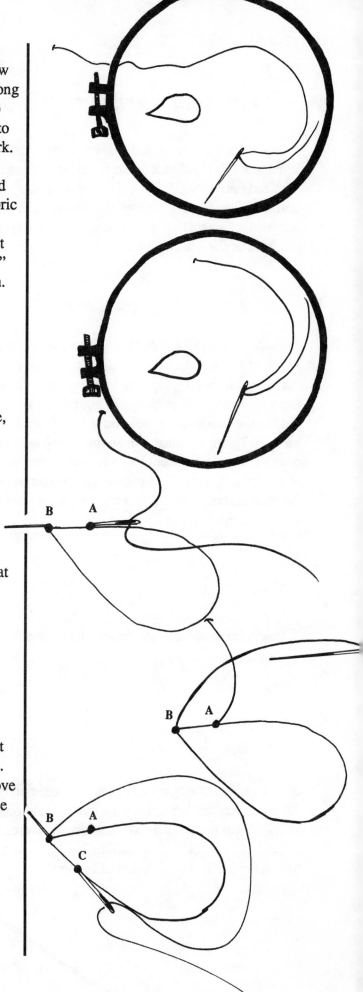

18

8. Thread below the needle, bring your needle down at (D) and up at (A).

9. Thread above the needle, bring your needle down at (E) and up at (C).

10. When you come to a large curve, make your outside stitches (on the largest part of the curve) larger. Make the inside stitches closer together. You may find it necessary, sometimes, to go in one hole twice on the inside area.

11. Keep turning your work so that the portion of stitching you are currently working on is horizontally in front of you and so that you are working left to right. This means that sometimes you will have the design upside down; however, just keep the section you are working on just like you would read the lines on a book. Horizontal and left to right.

12. When you have finished your work, weave the tail of the thread through the stitching on the sides. As with most needlework, never knot your thread. Just weave it.

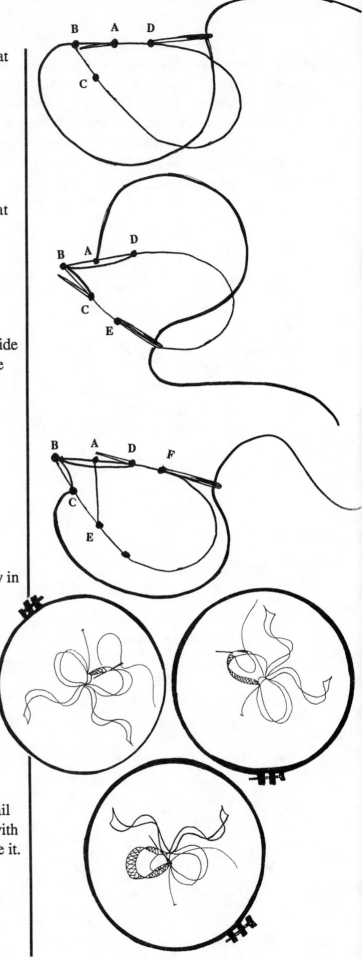

13. After you have finished either with a design or with the amount of floss you have in your needle, weave that end into the design. At that time, clip the knotted end which is either in the upper section of the fabric or held outside the embroidery hoop. Re-thread the needle with this end, and weave this end into the work as well.

(2)

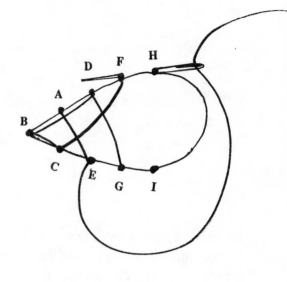

(1)

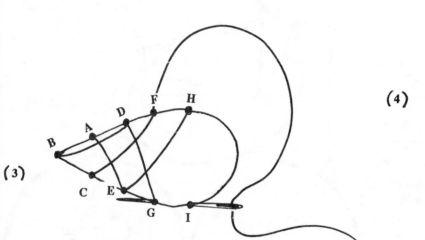

(4)

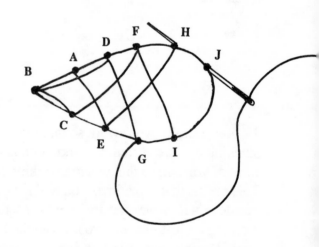

(3)

(6)

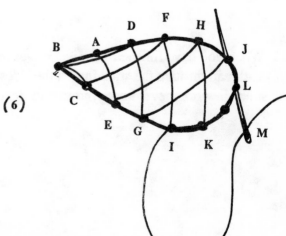

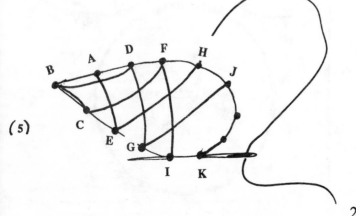

(5)

20

When I began teaching smocking, I found my students were very frustrated over an easy way to remember the rule, "When you move up, the thread is down; when you come down, the thread is up." For an experienced smocker, this is very simple to comprehend. For a beginner, remembering where to throw the thread is the most difficult concept to learn. Since the first fifteen years of my professional life were in teaching, I always try to make up something very simple or stupid or graphic to make a concept easy. In this case I wanted something so simple and silly that it simply could not be forgotten. The first time I made up this story, I was embarrassed to tell it. I thought, "Well, if they all get up and leave my shop during class, I will know that I can't use this story again." With fear and apprehension, I told my first "cat and the courthouse" story. If I remember correctly it was in a January 1982 smocking class with snow falling outside. Several years and over 1000 smocking students later, I can safely say that I am glad I made up the stupid story and more importantly, I am glad that I had the nerve to try it on the first class.

At this point maybe you are saying, "Hey, I bought this book to learn shadow work embroidery. Why is Martha talking about a smocking principle?" I will answer that question by saying that the floss position theory is the same with shadow work embroidery as it is with smocking. You will see.

SETTING: A courthouse in Huntsville, Alabama which has a long flight of steps leading to the door.
CHARACTERS: A Persian cat named Baby who has a very long tail. Martha Pullen who is the driver of the car.
TIME OF DAY: During business hours of Martha Pullen's Heirloom Shop at 518 Madison Street.

Martha Pullen has a Persian cat named Baby who wants to learn to drive a car. In order to drive this car, Baby must obtain a drivers license. Since Martha Pullen already has a license, Baby asks Martha to drive him to the courthouse so that he can take his test and obtain his license. Martha Pullen drives this cat to the courthouse. Martha opens the door and Baby jumps out of the car. Baby climbs to the top of the courthouse steps. He suddenly remembers that he forgot his money. Since you can't get a license without money, Baby must turn around and come back down the steps to the car. After turning around, Baby climbs down the long set of stairs until he reaches the car where Martha Pullen is waiting. He gets his money, turns back around again and climbs the steps to the door. The points in this ridiculous story which are applicable for smocking or shadow work embroidery are as follows:

1. The cat's tail symbolizes the thread of the shadow work or the smocking.

2. When a cat climbs up steep stairs, in which direction does her tail point? That's correct, down. The point to remember in shadow work embroidery or in smocking is that when you are moving to take a stitch—UP— the tail of the floss is down.

3. When a cat climbs down steep stairs, in which direction does her tail point? That's correct, up. The point to remember in shadow work embroidery or in smocking is that when you are moving to take a stitch—DOWNWARD—the tail of the floss is up.

4. Let me rephrase steps 2 and 3. (You surely know by this point in your life that all schoolteachers say everything at least three times before they quit explaining.) When the cat moves up the stairs, the tail is pointed down. When the cat moves down the stairs, the tail is pointed up.

5. Although this is not a smocking book, I will further point out what the story symbolizes. When the cat turns around at the top her tail swings around before she can begin to climb back down the stairs. That symbolizes a top cable before the wave or trellis moves downward. When the cat turns around at the bottom of the stairs to begin a move up again, that symbolizes a bottom cable before the climb back up. I just thought I would throw that in!

Mildred Turner's Method Of Shadow Work Embroidery

When my very close friend, Mildred Turner, discovered that I was writing a book on shadow work embroidery, she volunteered to write a chapter on "her way" of stitching shadow work embroidery. She knows that I prefer to stitch from the back; she prefers to stitch from the front. Here are her instructions for those of you who prefer to work from the front of the piece. Mildred has written two very marvelous books on heirloom sewing which also include shadow work embroidery designs. They can be ordered from Mimi's Smock Shoppe, 502 Balsam Rd., Hazelwood, NC 28738. (704) 452-3455

1. Trace the design very carefully onto the right side of the fabric. Use a very thin tracing line. Mildred prefers a chalk pencil. See **Fig. 1**.

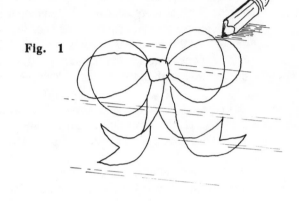

Fig. 1

2. Place the fabric into the hoop **right side up.** The design which you traced onto the fabric will be facing you. See **Fig. 2**.

Fig. 2

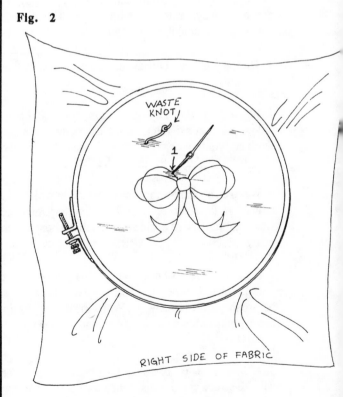

WASTE KNOT

1

RIGHT SIDE OF FABRIC

3. Cut a length of floss about 18" long and separate the strands of floss. Mildred prefers to iron her floss. First, separate several strands. Iron them by just pulling the floss under the iron.

4. Thread a #26 tapestry needle and knot the end of the thread.

22

5. Mildred likes using a waste knot since she can see where the end of the floss is located. She feels this gives her a better beginning stitch.

6. Leave a tail of floss about 2" long from the waste knot to the first stitch. The waste knot will be on the right side of the fabric.

7. Bring the needle to the right side where you wish to begin stitching. Refer to **Fig. 2.**

8. For your practice piece, refer to the bow in **Fig. 2.** The needle is brought up on the line at (1). The needle will enter at (2) and will be taken to the wrong side of the fabric. See **Fig. 3.**

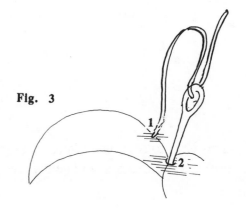

Fig. 3

9. Cross to the other line and bring the needle up at (3). Pull gently. See **Fig. 4.**

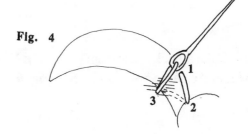

Fig. 4

10. Take a backstitch. The needle enters to the backside at (4). See **Fig. 5.**

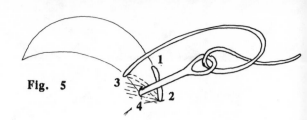

Fig. 5

11. Cross back to the other side where you first began, coming up at (5). See **Fig. 6.**

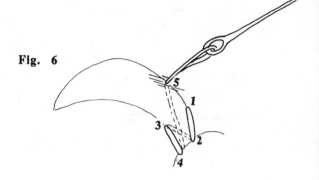

Fig. 6

12. Take a backstitch from (5) to (6). Notice that (6) was, at first, (2). See **Fig. 7.**

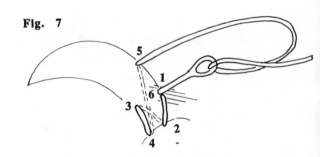

Fig. 7

13. Cross back to the second line, coming up at (7). Remember to pull your thread gently. See **Fig. 8**.

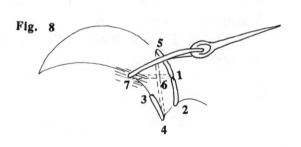

Fig. 8

14. Take a backstitch from (7) to (8). Notice that (8) shares the same hole as (3). See **Fig. 9**

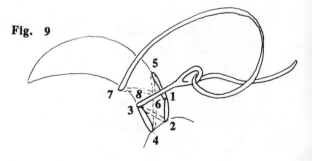

Fig. 9

24

15. Continue working in this manner until the design area is completely filled in. See **Fig. 10**. With the last stitch, the thread should be on the wrong side of the fabric. See **Fig. 11**.

16. Do not knot your thread to tie off. Finish by weaving the threaded needle along the edge of the stitch for about 1". Cut the thread. See **Fig. 12**.

17. Cut the waste knot off, thread your needle with the tail of thread and weave the needle along the other end to secure it. See **Fig 13**.

18. When coming to the points in the bow, refer to **Fig. 2**. Bring the needle up at (1). See **Fig. 14**.

19. Take the needle down at (2). This will also be the last stitch made before coming up at (1). See **Fig. 15**.

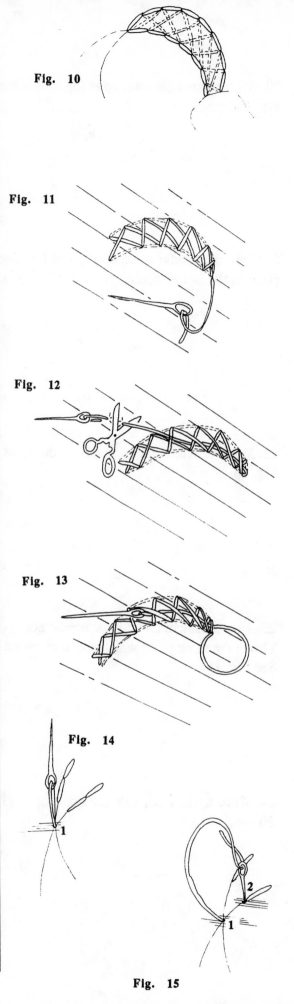

Fig. 10

Fig. 11

Fig. 12

Fig. 13

Fig. 14

Fig. 15

25

20. Bring the needle back up at (3), which was (1). See **Fig. 16.**

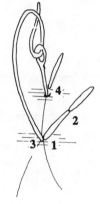

Fig. 16

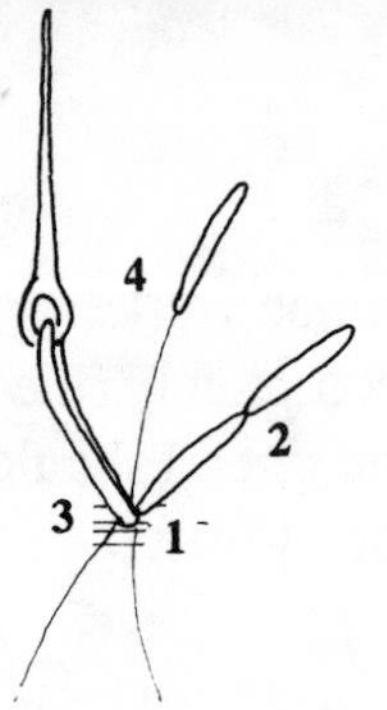

21. Take the needle down at (4), which is also the same point as the last stitch on that side. See **Fig. 17.**

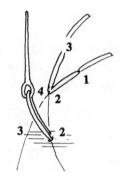

Fig. 17

22. Move forward and bring the needle up at (2). See **Fig. 18.**

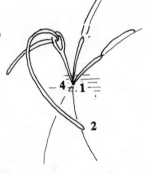

Fig. 18

23. Take a backstitch with the needle going down at (1). This is the same point which was used twice before. See **Fig. 19.**

Fig. 19

24. Move to the other side and come up at (3). See **Fig. 20.**

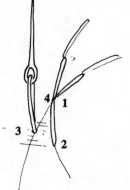

Fig. 20

25. Take a backstitch. The needle will again go down at (4). Remember (4) shares the same hole as (1). See **Fig. 21.**

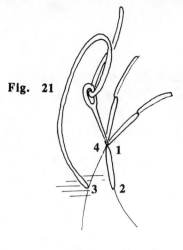

Fig. 21

26. Proceed as before, moving the needle forward and making back stitches. See **Fig. 22.**

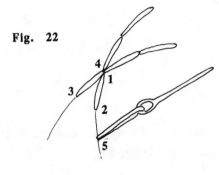

Fig. 22

27. When doing shadow work embroidery, there will be times when you will need to do just the backstitch for several stitches before beginning to do the shadow stitch again.

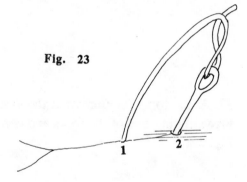

Fig. 23

28. To make a backstitch, bring the needle up at (1) and down at (2). See **Fig. 23.**

29. Move forward on the same line to (3). See **Fig. 24.**

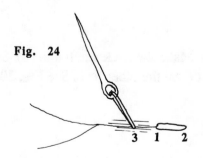

Fig. 24

27

30. Make the backstitch by entering at (4) which is also known as (1). See **Fig. 25.**

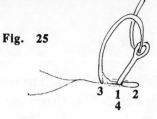

Fig. 25

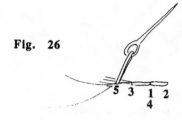

Fig. 26

31. Again, move forward on the same line and bring the needle up at (5). See **Fig. 26.**

Fig. 27

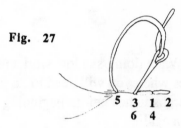

32. Make the backstitch entering at (6), which is also known as (3). See **Fig. 27.**

Fig. 28

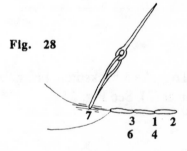

33. At the forks (beginning of the shadow) move forward onto one of the forks and come up at (7). See **Fig. 28.**

34. Make the back stitch into (8). See **Fig. 29.** Come up at (9) on the other fork. See **Fig. 30.**

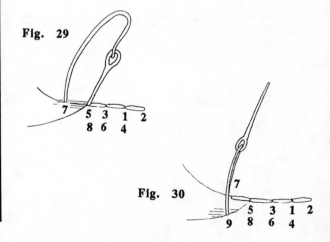

Fig. 29

Fig. 30

28

35. Do the backstitch by taking the needle down at (10), which used to be (8). See **Fig. 31.** And move forward to (11). See **Fig. 32.**

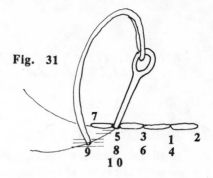

Fig. 31

36. Continue in this manner. The stitches should look like **Fig. 11** on the wrong side.

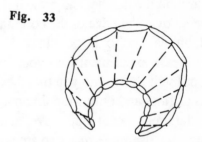

Fig. 32

37. When doing a shadow work embroidery design which is curved, (see **Fig. 33**) remember that the inner line of the curve is shorter than the outside line of a curve. You must compensate for this when you stitch. On the inside curve, make the stitches slightly shorter, while the backstitches on the outside curve will be slightly longer. Sometimes it may even be necessary to enter the same point twice.

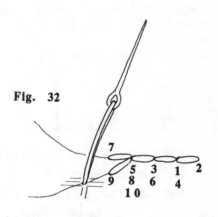

Fig. 33

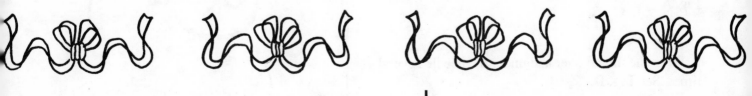

EMBROIDERY STITCH DIRECTIONS

Embroidery Tips

Here are some tips you might enjoy knowing from turn-of-the-century embroidery books.

1. If you don't like to use an embroidery hoop, use oilcloth and baste your work down on it.

2. Some people like to use two thimbles, one on the right hand and one on the left hand to protect the finger.

3. An emery bag will help to keep your needle smooth. An emery strawberry is available at most needlework departments.

4. Scissors with one sharp side and one blunt end are great for cutting thread on the wrong side.

French Knot

This little delicate beauty of a stitch is used in many places to embellish shadow work embroidery. There are several different theories concerning the French knot. Some say if you wrap the knot more than once, it becomes a bullion. After doing research through many embroidery books, I find that this is not the case. From a Butterick Transfer book dated 1917, I find the following description of a French knot.

"Bring the thread up and take an ordinary backstitch. Wind the thread once, twice or three times around the needle, and draw it through, holding the coil down with the left thumb. Then, insert the needle over the edge of the coil in the same hole, thus making the knot secure. Do not cut the thread, but pass on to the next knot."

Please experiment with your French knots. After consulting with Margaret Boyles and Judith Dobson, I will share with you that they both prefer making a larger French knot by using more strands of floss and only wrapping once. They say that more than one wrap with one strand of floss makes the French knot topple over and become loose. You might want to try wrapping the needle just once and use more than one strand of floss. A little texture can be added with a few knots placed on the work. French knots can be used to fill in areas such as the center of flowers for a very lovely effect. Use a #10 crewel needle.

Steps For French Knot With Several Wraps Of Thread:

1. Bring thread to the top of the work out at (1). See **Fig. A**

2. Wrap the thread over and under the needle several times. See **Fig. D.**

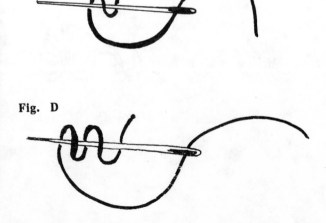

Fig. A

Fig. D

3. Hold the wraps and pull the needle through until you can push the needle back down into the fabric (2) at almost the same place you came out originally. See **Fig. B.** Finished French knot is illustrated by **Fig. E.**

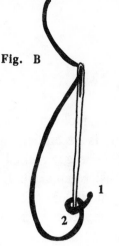

Fig. B

4. You may pass the thread behind the fabric to the next French knot if your fabric is not sheer. However, when you are stitching shadow work embroidery, you will usually use a thin fabric. Therefore, it is best to tie off the French knot before passing to the next one. The pass threads will not be pretty peeking from behind thin fabric.

Fig. E

Steps For French Knot With One Wrap Around The Needle:

1. Push the needle through the fabric from the back. Come out at (1). See **Fig. A.**

Fig. A   1

2. Holding the needle in your right hand, place the needle in a horizontal position above the thread. See **Fig. A.**

3. Holding the floss in your left hand, wrap the floss around the needle one time. Go under the needle first and over the needle second.

Fig. B

4. With the point of the needle, go back through the fabric at (2). See **Fig. B.** This is almost the exact same place as (1); just move over at least a thread of the fabric.

5. A finished, one-wrap, French knot is illustrated by **Fig. C.**

Fig. C

Bullion Knot

One of the favorite stitches for embellishing shadow work embroidery is the bullion knot. It is exquisite for making roses, large or small. Some people seem to think that is it easier to make bullion knots while the hoop is in an embroidery frame so that you can use both hands to manipulate the needle and thread. Use a #10 crewel needle.

Steps For Bullion Knot:

1. Push the needle through the fabric from the back of your work. Come out at (1). See **Fig. A**.

2. Bring the needle in at (2), creating the length of the bullion that you want. **Do not pull your floss though.** See **Fig. A**.

3. Bring the needle out again into the same hole at (1). Pass only three quarters of the needle through the fabric. See **Fig. B**.

4. Right hand holding the needle, left hand wrapping the floss, begin to wrap the loose floss in a counter-clockwise direction around the needle. See **Fig C**. Wrap it the number of times you need for the length bullion you want. For a short bullion wrap about 5 times. For a longer bullion, wrap 13, 15, or even 19 times. Experiment at all levels in between the 5-wrap and the 19-wrap to see the lengths which are possible.

5. Slide the wraps down on the needle. Move the wraps close to the eye of the needle. Hold the wraps in place with your left thumb and index finger. See **Fig. D**.

6. Still holding the wraps with your left hand, carefully pull the needle up with your right hand. The rest of the floss will pass through the wraps. See **Fig. E**.

7. Arrange your bullion exactly right. See **Fig. E**.

8. Finish the bullion by pushing the needle into the back of the fabric near the last coil (2). See **Fig. F**.

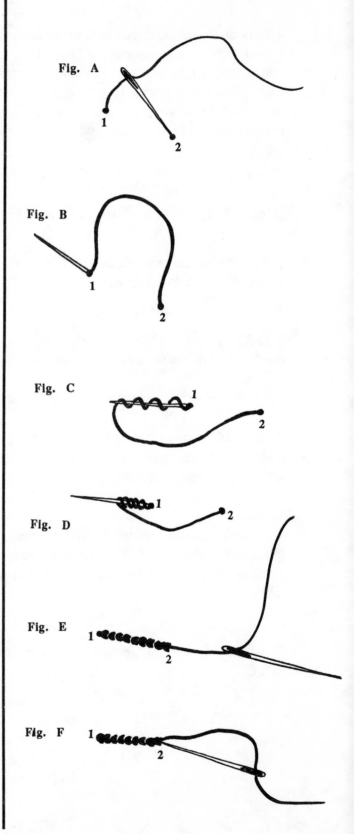

Fig. A

Fig. B

Fig. C

Fig. D

Fig. E

Fig. F

Backstitch

This technique makes a continuous line of stitches.

Steps For Backstitch:

1. Bring the thread through the fabric at (1). See **Fig. A.**

2. Make a small backward stitch at (2). See **Fig. A.**

3. Bring the needle up again in front of the first stitch (3) and take it back down again through the original insertion point (1). See **Fig. A.** The needle always emerges one stitch ahead, ready to make the next backstitch.

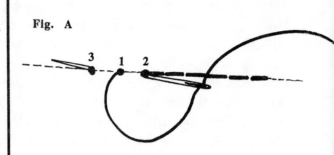

Fig. A

Stem Stitch Or Outline Stitch

This stitch is worked from left to right. It makes a line of slanting stitches. The thread is kept to the left and below the needle. Make small, even stitches. The needle is inserted just below the line to be followed, comes out to the left of it, and above the line, slightly.

Steps In Stem (or Outline) Stitch:

1. Come up from behind at (1). See **Fig. A.**

2. Go down into the fabric again at (2). This is a little below the line.

3. Come back up at (3). This is a little above the line. Keep the thread below the needle.

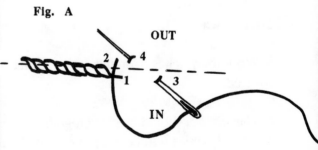

Fig. A

Outlining and Padding Stitches

The outlining of a pattern is very important before making a satin stitch over it. Use the directions for stem stitch found on the previous page. Make the stitches even and on the line. Padding before satin stitching means just that. Fill in the outline in length-wise stitches with uneven darning stitches, taking short stitches on the wrong side and longer stitches on the right side. Make them close together. If a raised effect is desired, make three or four thicknesses of padding stitches. Keep the padding even, making it higher in the center and spreading the stitches more toward the edge. Several strands of darning cotton are used for padding. See **Fig. B.**

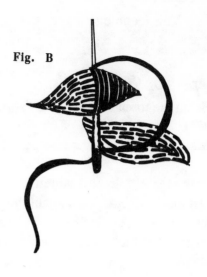

Fig. B

Satin Stitch

Basic satin stitch dates back for centuries. Satin stitch basically covers a whole shape. Use one or two strands of floss. This is a stitch which takes some practice to make pretty. You can work satin stitch either straight or on the diagonal.

Steps In Satin Stitch:

1. Bring the needle out at (1). See **Fig. A.**

2. Go down at (2).

3. Work the stitches over and over until the shape is covered.

4. The stitches should be close together, but should not overlap. Practice will be necessary to make them smooth and even.

5. Gradually, lengthen or shorten each stitch to conform to the shape you are making.

6. The edges of the shape should be kept neat; the stitches at a reasonable length.

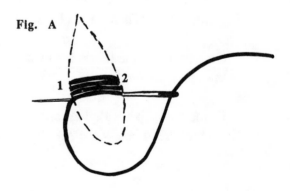

Fig. A

Lazy Daisy Stitch

This little delicate stitch gets its name because it looks like a daisy.

Steps In Lazy Daisy Stitch:

1. Bring the needle through the fabric at the inner point of the petal (1). See **Fig. A.**

2. Insert again at almost the same point, but just a thread away (2). See **Fig. A.**

3. Take a stitch toward the large loop of the daisy (the outside of the petal), with the thread looped under the needle.

4. Hold the loop with a small stitch (3). See **Fig. B.**

5. Bring the needle back in again at the center of the inner point of the petal. See **Fig. A.**

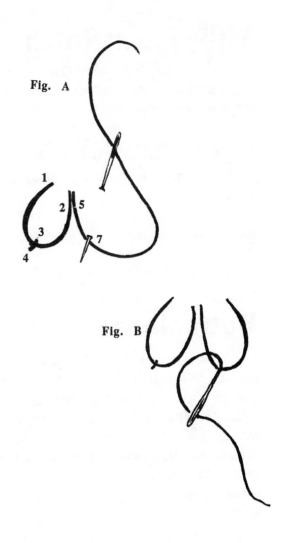

Fig. A

Fig. B

Eight-Strand Stitch

This pretty stitch is another form of a flower stitch. Use four strands of floss.

Steps In Eight-Strand Stitch:

1. Thread your needle with four strands of floss.

2. Bring the needle up at (1) which is the inner part of the petal. See **Fig. A.**

3. Insert the needle down at (2) which is the outer end of the petal. See **Fig. A.**

4. Bring the needle up in the inner end of the next petal. See **Fig. A**

5. Do not pull too tightly. Spread the floss out a little bit with either your fingernail or the blunt end of your needle.

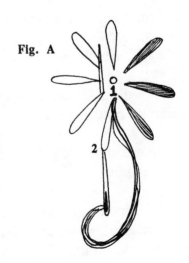

Fig. A

Mille Fleur Stitch

Use a single strand of floss for this stitch. You might want to experiment with a denser weight of floss which is more "rope like."

Steps For Mille Fleur Stitch

1. Work from the inner point (1) to the outer point (2). See **Fig. A.**

2. Stitch from the inner point to the outer point.

3. Come up again at the center point.

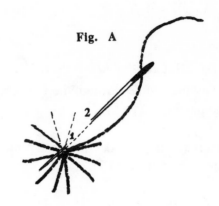

Fig. A

Buttonhole Stitch

This stitch is worked from left to right and two lines are followed. It is especially pretty when you want to work a buttonhole scallop around the edge of a collar. Hold the work secure in a hoop or by basting onto an oilcloth if you do not like to use a hoop. The older embroidery books suggest filling in the scalloped areas with small stitches such as a running stitch. This would be done before you begin your buttonhole scallops.

Steps For Buttonhole Stitch:

1. Work from left to right.

2. Begin to buttonhole at the extreme left.

3. Insert the needle at the lower edge (1). See **Fig A.**

4. Insert the needle at (2) and bring in at (3). The thread is held under the needle. See **Fig. A.**

4. Pass the thread under the point and draw the needle through. See **Fig. B.**

5. The needle is inserted a little to the right on the upper line, taken straight downwards behind the work to come out on the lower line over the thread. The thread is then pulled to form a loop. See **Fig. B.**

6. Keep them close together and curve them to make a scallop. See **Fig. C.**

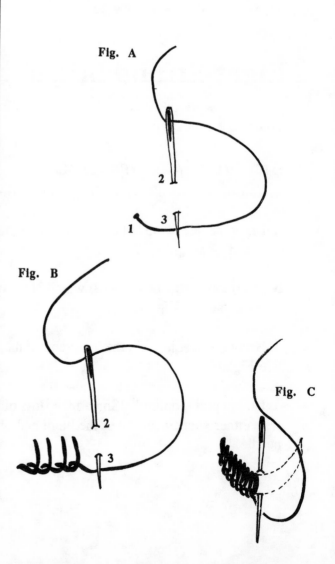

Fig. A

Fig. B

Fig. C

Chain Stitch

The chain stitch can be worked in a straight row, on a curve, or inside as a filler stitch. If the chain stitch is to be used as a filler stitch, work from the outside of the design to the inside. Place each row parallel to the other row of chain stitch which is right beside it.

Steps For Chain Stitch:

1. Bring the thread from below the fabric at (1). See **Fig. A.**

2. Holding the thread to the left of the needle, go back into the same hole at (1) forming a loop by holding the thread with your left thumb.

3. Bring the needle out at (2). Keep the thread under the needle. This forms a loop.

4. If you are making a curved chain stitch just take your needle to the right or left to form a curve. See **Fig. B.**

Feather Stitch

I used to think you could tell poor embroidery from excellent embroidery by the quality of a woman's feather stitch! I still put a great deal of faith in this stitch. It is lovely for borders, stems, branches and leaf fillings. I will give you a quick "cheat" trick at this time. If your sewing machine has a feather stitch on it, run the feather stitch, **without any thread,** anywhere you want your hand featherstitch. Then, just work your hand featherstitch in those holes.

Steps For Feather Stitch:

1. Bring your needle from behind your work (1). See **Fig. A.**

2. Working at an angle, and holding the thread to make a loop, go down again at (2) and back up at (3). Be sure you pass the needle over the thread. That is what forms the feather. See **Fig. B.**

3. Move over at another angle (4) and repeat. See **Fig. C.**

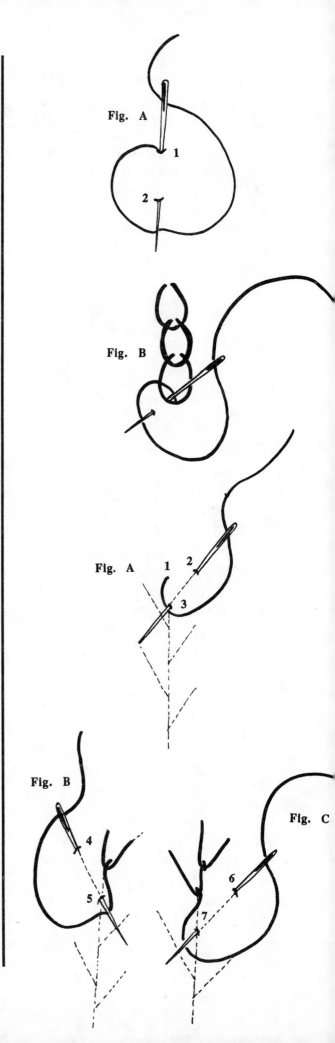

37

Embroidered Elegance
by Tina Taylor McEwen

Your response to Tina McEwen's dress designs in the Winter 1989 *Sew Beautiful* issue prompted me to ask her to sketch some more ideas for your sewing creativity. This time Tina was asked to design the dress with a specific embroidery design in mind. Our staff squealed over the results; we hope you do also. Enjoy! I might add that each of these dresses could be made very inexpensively if domestic batiste is used. Actually, since the embroidery is by hand, any one of these dresses would not be too expensive even if made with Swiss batiste!

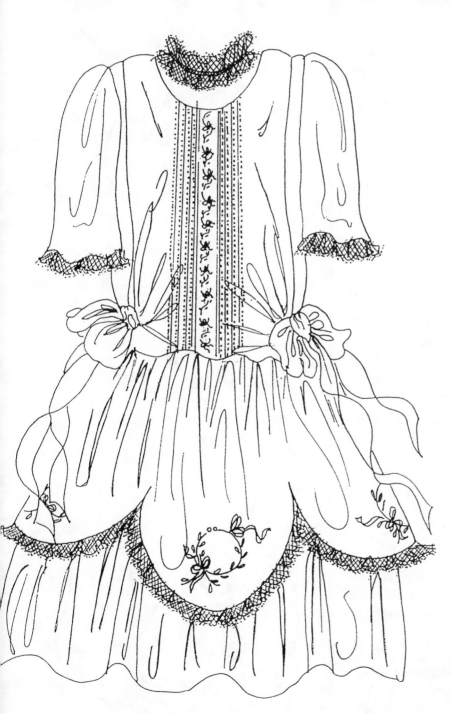

Suzanne

Such sophistication for the older girl or for you! This basic scoop neck, dropped waist dress has such an interesting skirt. Don't you think that this double skirt would only be pretty on a low waisted dress. We would love it on high waisted yoke dress for little girls and on a to the waist dress for all ages. It would be pretty in batiste, silk, or handkerchief linen. As on most of the "creative front designs" make the tucks and stitch the embroidery before cutting out the dress. The embroidery is especially lovely on this one and includes shadow work bows, bullion roses in the bow, outline stitched stems, French knots and lazy daisy leaves. More of the same stitches are placed in the circle for the coordinating embroidery on the scallops of the skirt. Two pieces of 2" edging has been gathered and stitched onto a 1/4" matching ribbon; this ties in the back for a truly Victorian lace necklace. The large bows are either of self fabric or ribbon.

Morgan

So sweet for summer months as a dress and for winter months as a pinafore is Morgan, our second dress and embroidery design. We call this skirt shape, Cathedral Window, because of the look. Each arched shape is made large enough for the elegant little shadow embroidery, bullion rosebud, stem stitch, French knots, and satin stitch flowers design to fit right inside. Lace insertion is stitched on top of a straight skirt; edging is gathered slightly and stitched around the insertion. Stitch the lace edging on one side only so that the other side is unattached to the dress. The bottom of the dress is lovely and simple with one row of lace insertion with one row of flat lace edging attached to that. The front and back of the pinafore has about 25 1/2" tucks. We suggest using Sarah Howard Stone's "Bijoux" as a guideline for this type of dress. You could also use any round yoke dress pattern using the bottom of the yoke for your guide. There isn't an exact pattern for this exact dress. This skirt (Cathedral Window) lace treatment would be lovely on any skirt of almost any dress.

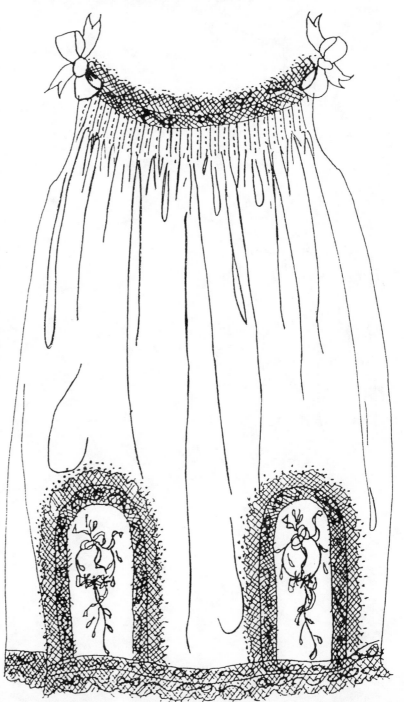

Lindsay

Embroidery, tucks, lace, and a 10" wide fabric sash make this beauty one to savor forever. Tina has designed a garland which would be stem or outline stitched. The bullion rosebuds are spaced evenly; the lazy daisy leaves are also pretty. Scatter shadow work butterflies anywhere you would like to see one! Choose your favorite dropped waist dress pattern. Ours is "Victorian Middy Dress" by Martha Pullen. Before you cut out your bodice, make a flat piece of tucked fabric following Tina's guidelines. She used 6 1/4" tucks on each side with 9 1/4" tucks about twice as long in the center. After making your dress front, lay your pattern on top of the tucked piece and cut. The very full sleeves are gathered around the elbow. The self ruffle is below the elbow. Elastic is used to gather the sleeves. On top of that elastic is a "ribbon garland by the yard" trim which features green leaves and ribbon rosettes. This should be stitched on by hand after the elastic is sewn into the sleeve. Give enough room for the child to get her hand into the sleeve. The garland of hand embroidery is found on the bottom of each sleeve and again on the bottom of the skirt. We think this dress would be absolutely gorgeous in white or any very pale color of Swiss batiste, namely Oriunda or Nelona. Try using an Imperial batiste slip of a contrasting color underneath the white Swiss dress or the ecru Swiss dress. Perhaps you could choose the slip color to match any of your chosen colors of the embroidery. The gathered collar has been hand embroidered to match the rest of the garment.

40

Ann

What an imaginative idea for a tailored and fancy dress all wrapped up in one package! Use any square collared pattern; our favorite is the "Pre-Teen Classic Dress" which was in the Spring 1989 issue of *Sew Beautiful*. Add the center piece of the collar and stitch to your heart's content. This dress would be lovely in any fabric-linen, batiste, silk, calico, broadcloth-just pick your favorite. The three tiny tucks finish the lower edge of the sleeve. The bias band lends itself nicely to gathered lace which has been whipped on to form that little fancy touch. The three tucks on the skirt are elegant and tailored; the bottom of the skirt is finished nicely with straight lace edging. Use any kind of sash you like; however, please make the bow large and wonderful. The embroidery design for this collar consists of shadow embroidered large leaves, lazy daisy small leaves, eyelets, French knots, and stem stitch vines. The dress might be of one fabric, like batiste, and the collar of linen. We love handkerchief linen for embroidery. Another lovely option for the collar would be organdy. As a matter of fact, the whole dress would be pretty in organdy.

41

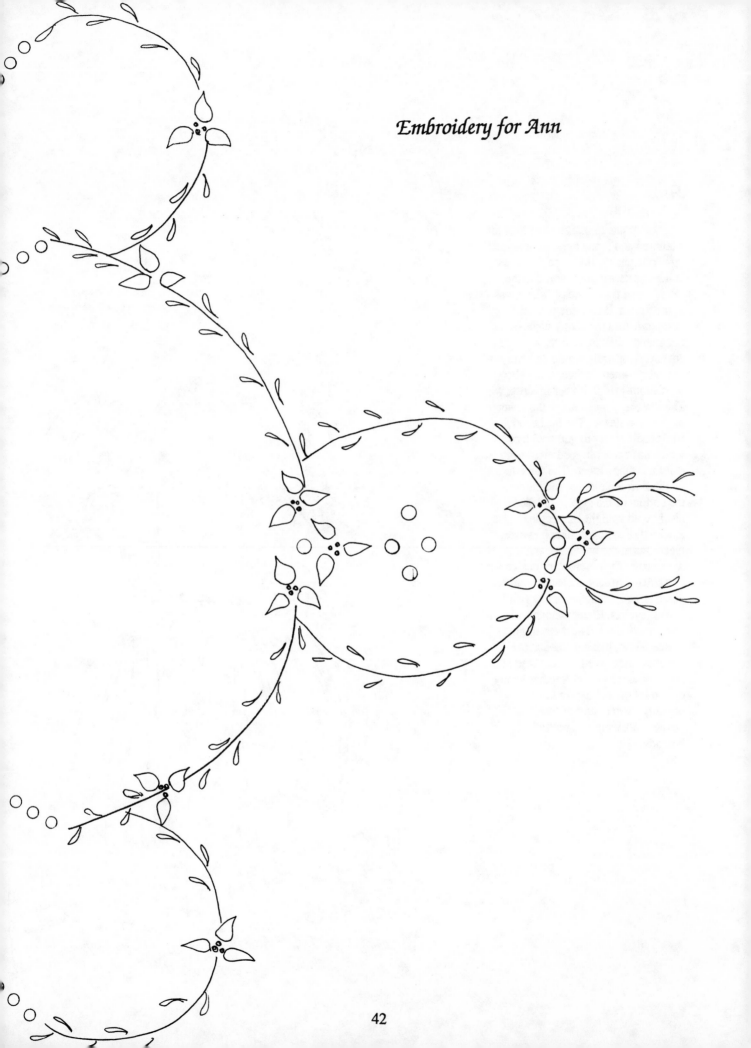

Embroidery for Ann

Mary

What a lovely idea for a French bishop with tiny touches of shadow embroidery. To make this dress, use your favorite bishop pattern, and cut angel sleeves for the dress. Lace trim is used on the edge of the sleeves, the edge of the angel sleeves and the bottom of the dress. The shadow bows should be embroidered before the sleeves are cut out and before the skirt is cut if you are going to put the bows very close to the bottom of the skirt. The collar consists of three layers of Swiss batiste edged with lace. The Victorian neckline is made by stitching three layers of insertion together and finishing with gathered lace edging. The wide satin bows are lovely on the shoulders!

The shadow work designs on this page were contributed by Mildred Turner. Thanks, Mildred! (Art by Rebekah Russell.) For more beautiful embroidery designs see Mimi's Heirloom Sewing books, I and II. Mimi's Smock Shoppe, Inc., 502 Balsam Rd., Hazelwood, N.C. 28738, (704) 452-3455

The shadow work designs on this page were contributed by Mildred Turner. Thanks, Mildred! (Art by Rebekah Russell.) For more beautiful embroidery designs see Mimi's Heirloom Sewing books, I and II. Mimi's Smock Shoppe, Inc., 502 Balsam Rd., Hazelwood,

The shadow work designs on this page were contributed by Mildred Turner. Thanks, Mildred! (Art by Rebekah Russell.) For more beautiful embroidery designs see Mimi's Heirloom Sewing books, I and II. Mimi's Smock Shoppe, Inc., 502 Balsam Rd., Hazelwood, N.C. 28738, (704) 452-3455

687

3607

913

326

913

819

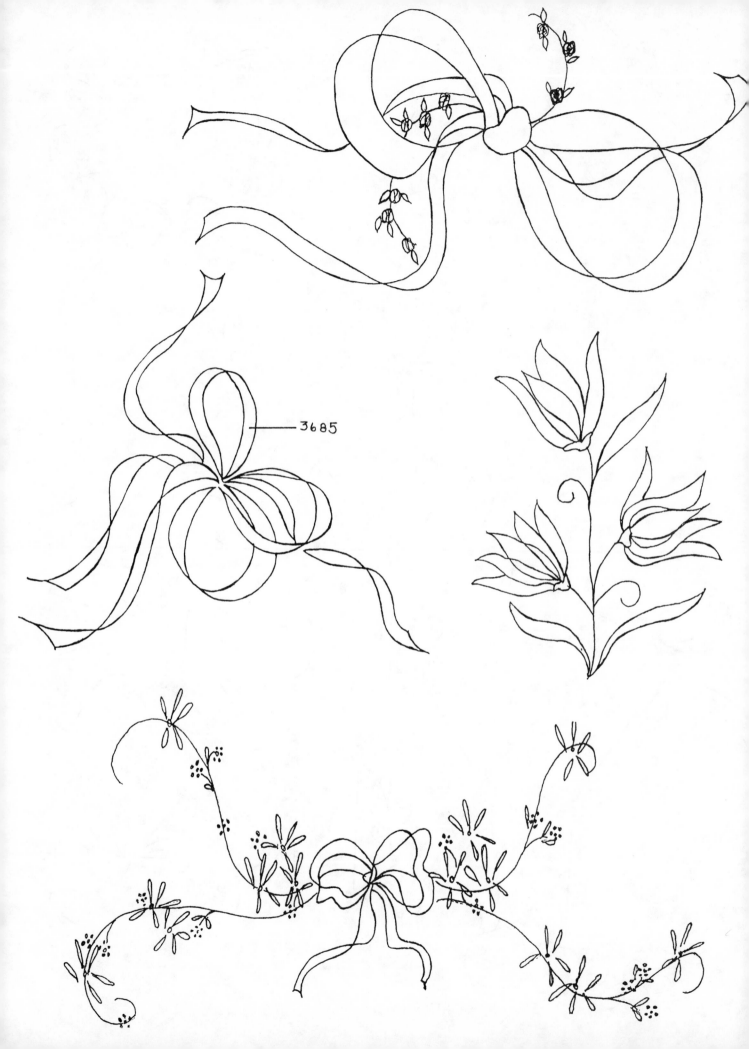

3685

992

3687

3687
553
3688

3687
3688

553

553

369

3687

992

518

747

828

351

742

353

943

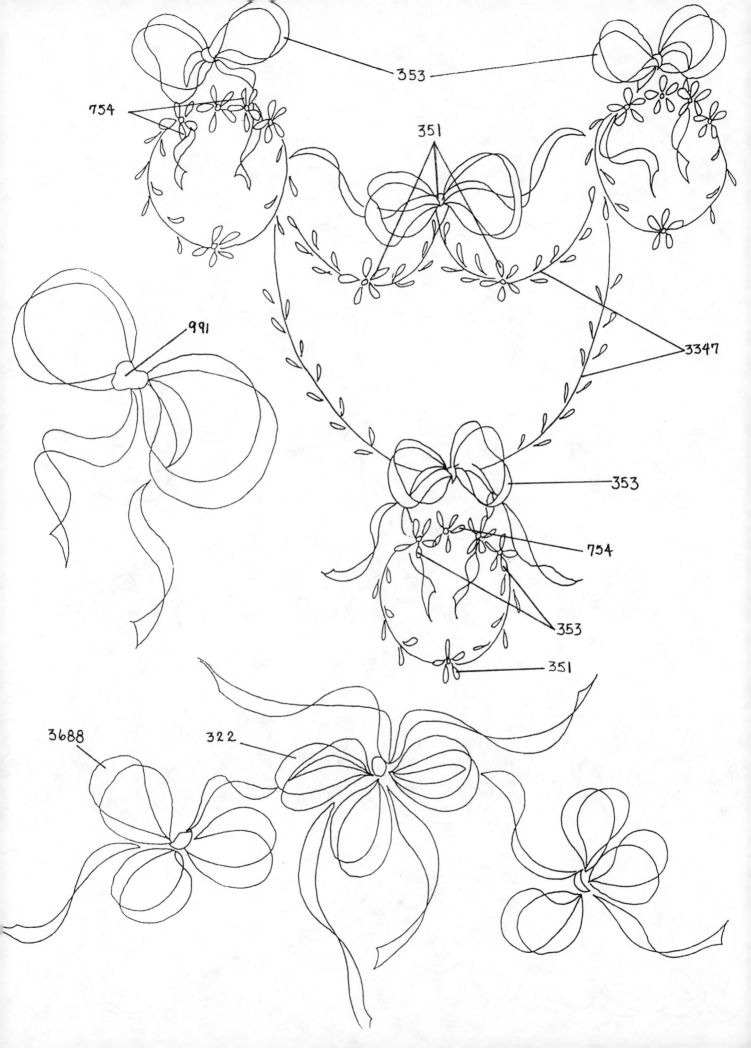

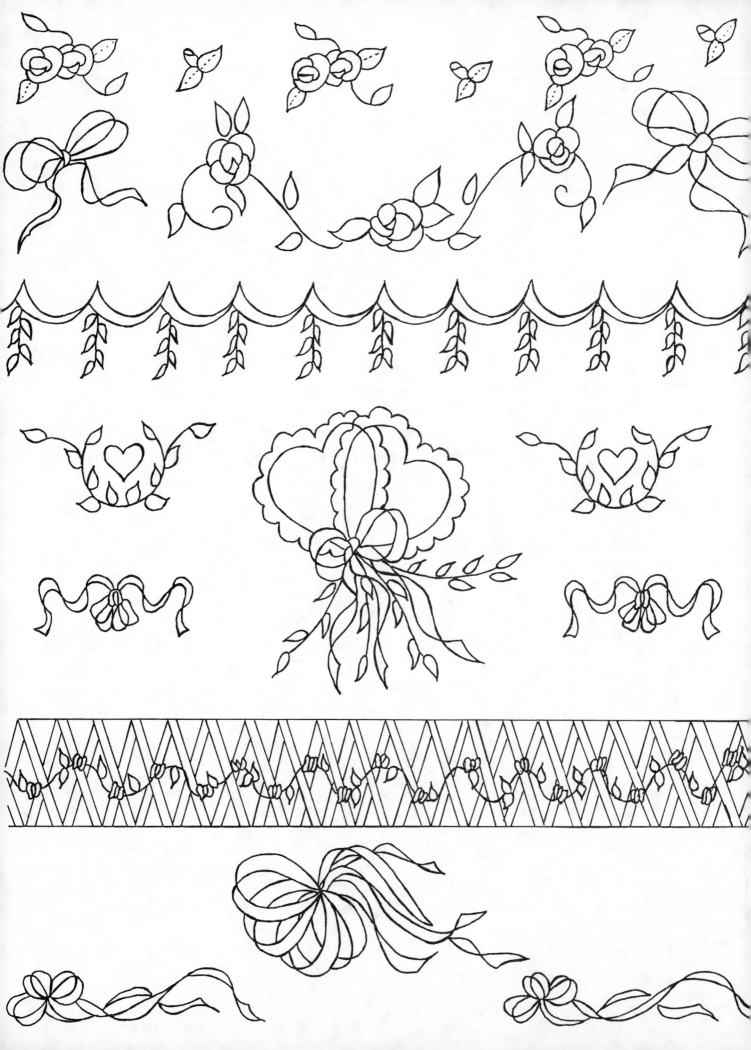

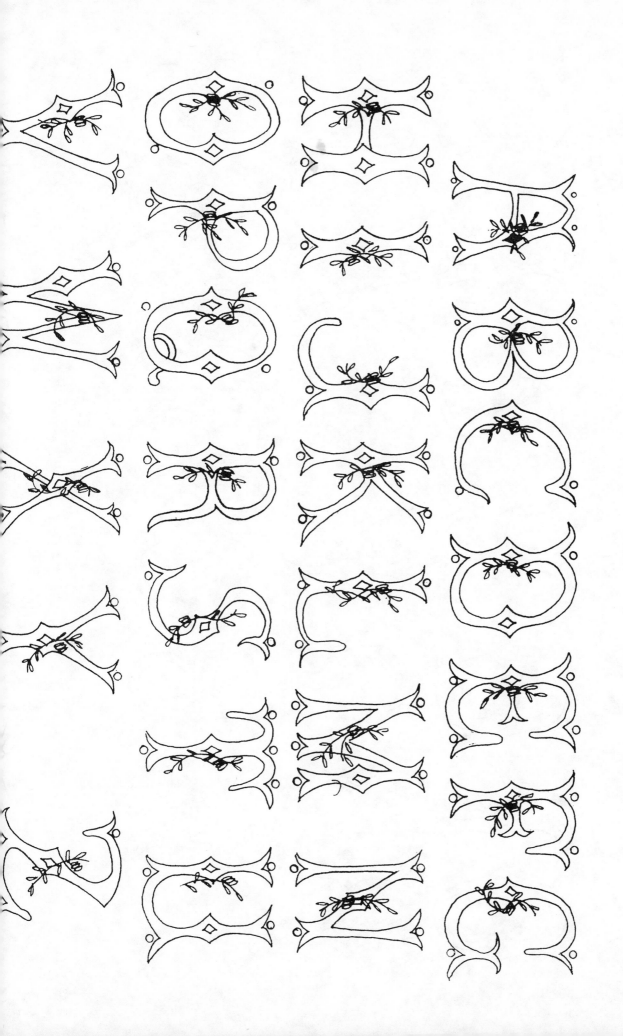

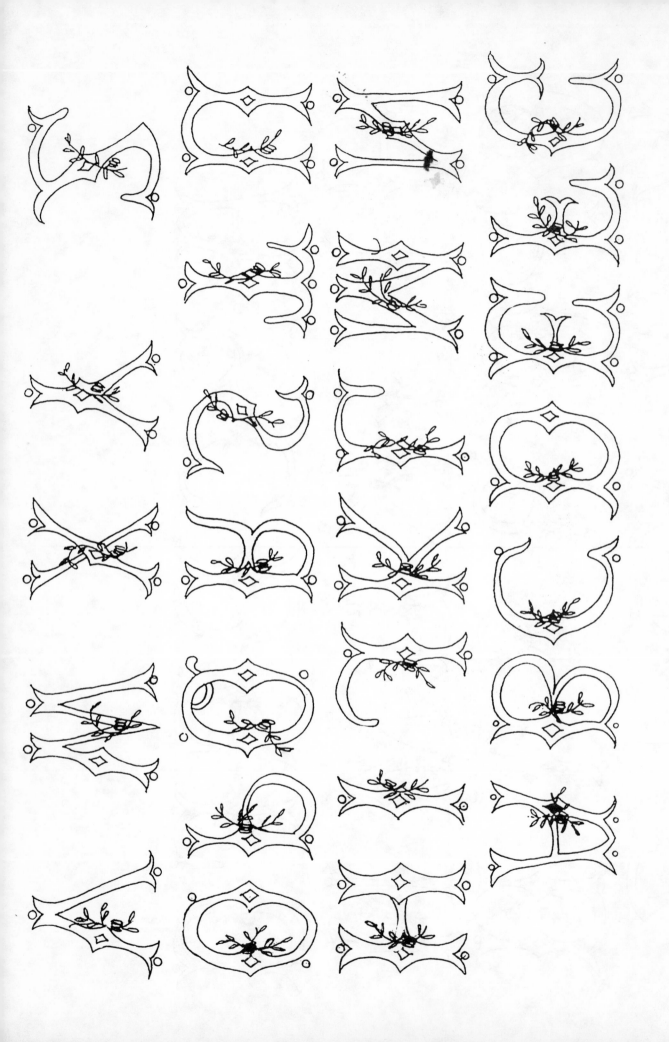